SHORTCOMINGS

OF

THE PURITAN CHURCH,

AND

REORGANIZATION OF SOCIETY.

BY

JEROME B. HOLGATE,

AUTHOR OF "NOACHIDAE," AND DISCOVERER OF THE LAWS OF HISTORY.

NEW YORK:
BAKER & GODWIN, PRINTERS AND PUBLISHERS,
PRINTING-HOUSE SQUARE, OPPOSITE CITY HALL.
Sold by Booksellers generally.
1863.

SINGLE COPY, 25 CTS.; FIVE COPIES, $1; FIFTY COPIES, $8; ONE HUNDRED COPIES, $14; ONE THOUSAND COPIES FOR $100.

SHORTCOMINGS

OF

THE PURITAN CHURCH

AND

REORGANIZATION OF SOCIETY.

BY

JEROME B. HOLGATE,

AUTHOR OF "NOACHIDAE," AND DISCOVERER OF THE LAWS OF HISTORY.

NEW YORK:
BAKER & GODWIN, PRINTERS AND PUBLISHERS,
PRINTING-HOUSE SQUARE, OPPOSITE CITY HALL.
Sold by Booksellers generally.
1863.

SHORTCOMINGS.

Puritanism was a protest against errors in doctrine, and a purification of the church from an ostentatious ritual; but in its anxiety to establish Evangelical Christianity, it went off in another direction, and lugged in many things equally useless, absurd, and calculated to inflict upon the church serious and grievous wounds. Its errors, however, were more those of the head than of the heart, and are to be ascribed in a great measure to the age in which it originated. At that time the intellect was exceedingly limited in its conception of what ought to constitute the true landmarks and boundaries between our spiritual and worldly obligations, and therefore it clothed the central truth of Christianity—salvation by faith—with a wretched caricature rather than the beautiful garments of a pure taste and a sound judgment.

Why should the church, in ignoring priestcraft and kingcraft, assume other burthens as absurd as those she deprecated? Our objections to her, therefore, are the following: While she pleaded for *justification* by faith, she neglected the Law and the Prophets.

She accused Rome of having violated and abridged the decalogue, and then superseded it with her own ordinances, and, at the same time, she, herself, subjoined thereto a host of trivial inventions, equally objectionable and ridiculous; for example, she added the following *trivialities* to the solemn specifications of the law: Thou shalt not go to a horse-race. Thou shalt not go to a party. Thou shalt not go to a ball. Thou shalt not go to a theatre. Thou shalt not play cards, drafts, nor chess. Thou shalt look exceedingly long-faced, gloomy, and severe!

We say nothing of the blue laws of Connecticut, for it is very doubtful whether they are genuine, and the Christian religion has been caricatured enough without these. Some of us, for ten years, have heard regular denunciations from the pulpit against attending theatres and similar amusements, as though these were the fundamental sins of the decalogue, while sitting in the presence of the preacher were professors of religion who were in the daily habit of breaking the commandments, and not a word of rebuke uttered by the preacher in that direction! Such failure in the performance of the ministerial duties, and such perversion of the mission of Christ's ambassadors from publishing the law and the penalty to the proclamation of their own prejudices, was calculated to bring the church into derision, and to lead, in the end, to the corruption of public morals, by leaving to flourish, in unrestrained vigor, those passions which it is the object of Christianity to overcome and crush out!

She has neglected to assail with her whole power, and with the fearful threatenings of God's wrath, the violation of the commandment, "Thou shalt not covet," till the entire population seems to be insane with the spirit of covetousness, and is, at this moment, rocking under this mighty passion with a violence that threatens the dissolution of the political fabric! What branch of business is not corrupted by it? What office in the Government is not sought after and wrangled for, for the purpose of gratifying its insatiable cravings? What corruption in all our corporations, railroad and banking? What fraud and imposition in our manufacturing establishments? And what dishonesty and malfeasance in the officials of these establishments?

She has neglected to proclaim, with her whole strength, the penalty of God's wrath against the violation of the commandment, "Thou shalt not bear false witness against thy neighbor," until the constant practice, on the part of the press, of violating this commandment, is shocking to every mind of pure feeling and noble instinct—dealing in slander, vituperation, and misrepresentation to such an extent that the public mind, instead of being enlightened, is only blinded and bewildered by it; and it indulges the monstrous delusion of supposing that this is its regular mission, and that it is not criminal in so doing, and will not be brought to judgment for it. The scandal and insinuation against character indulged in, in the social circle, which it is needless to mention is another infraction of this commandment, is nothing compared with this withering violation of it in the very fountains of our political life.

She has neglected to hold up before the nation the terrible law, "Thou shalt not steal." Some of us have lived long enough to know the origination of the political party cry, "To the victor belong the spoils;" and the adoption of the motto, "A northern man with southern principles;" yet the one advocating the appropriation of offices by mere partisans, without reference to their worthiness or capacity, and insinuating robbery and stealing, till now it seems to be imagined there is no disparagement in plundering the public treasury; the other political *hypocrisy*; yet, during the whole period since, have not heard a solitary sermon from the pulpit condemning these monstrous political principles, until the Government explodes with fearful violence, and a horde of official thieves and plunderers makes its sudden exit from the capital!!

She has not labored to repress the spirit of ambition and rivalry in the nation; that is to say, to bring to bear against it the power of the pulpit.

The practice of teaching boys to rival their schoolmates in their studies, and the system of promoting pupils at the head or foot of the class according as they excel in their studies in the lower, and the rewards and honors bestowed upon them in our higher, literary institutions, is only one way of inculcating a spirit of rivalry and ambition,—at least, we would suggest, whether it is not so,—strengthening and invigorating the baser passions, which ought to be repressed and subdued. The consequence is, our entire population is striving to outwit each other in acquiring property or office, and employing every kind of chicanery, strategy, and trickery for the attainment of these ends, considering it as evidence of smartness, and commendable rather than as deserving of condemnation, till finally the noble-minded are disgusted with the scramble for office or the love of gain which devours the souls of this people. The result is, that money and power are exalted above genius and worth, and the nation reels under the force of passions which it was the mission of the church to overcome, destroy, and crush out.

She systematically discourages or neglects the study of the prophecies, thereby depriving her congregations of that support and strength to their faith which is derived from a consciousness of God's sovereignty in the world, and the knowledge which is necessary to keep up that spirit of watchfulness so earnestly recommended by the Saviour as necessary to prevent their being taken unawares by his second coming. She thus ignores the glorious privilege of being reckoned among those whom the angel declares shall at the time of the end understand Daniel's visions, and whom the apocalyptic angel pronounces "blessed," for reading and keeping the sayings of the Book of Revelation.

The result is, she is in the condition of the Sardisan church; she has *received* the prophets, but does not study them, and consequently does not *watch*, and she therefore loses sight of *the judgment-day* and of the punishment for sin—of *the resurrection-day*, and of the rewards of the righteous—and she seems to imagine she has done her duty when she enjoins attendance on church on the Sabbath, great gravity of deportment, profound respect for the Bible generally, and giving her dozy congregations good moral discourses which, on the whole, compare very well with most of those of deistical writers; and the compositions of some of our school-boys, so far as sentiment is concerned, containing about as much; hardly outstripping the ancient philosophers in this respect; falling into a vague deism, neological in character; cold and lifeless in spirit, as a general thing; infatuated with gorgeous churches, as though she would veil her spiritual barrenness in external robes of splendor; her worshipers scarcely recognizable from men of the world, so worldly are they in their conduct; astonished if any allusion is made to Christ's second coming, or the judgment-day, or the resurrection-day; seeming to regard religion rather as a *fine* sentiment, than a deadly grapple with our depraved natures, the issues of which are life or death!

How is it possible under these circumstances and in this state of things for *the believer* to preserve himself pure and unspotted from the world? Where is his higher spiritual nature to find sympathy and aliment when it is constantly wounded by coming in contact with unmitigated depravity? He feels that the practical development of Christianity thus far is not in accordance with the demands of his higher nature, and he feels the want of sympathy and support in any attempt which he may make to realize the conceptions of his own mind on the subject, and concludes to abandon it and float along with the great current of human passion and corruption and do the best he can.

Still, in her day the Puritan Church has been the salt of the earth; but she needs vitalizing or reforming.

REORGANIZATION OF SOCIETY.

THE modern style of church building has originated in comparatively modern times, and the Puritan method of *sermonizing* has sprung from the age of discussion, when men fought over doctrines and matters of faith, and does not propperly belong to the worship of the Christian church. The temple is the true Bible style of architecture.

It is proposed to build, in the city of New York, a magnificent and beautiful Temple, and also others in other parts of the continent, all eventually to be connected with the great Temple, which is to be erected at Jerusalem. Temples will also be built in various parts of Europe and in Asia, forming a chain of temples round the globe!

A burning globe of light might be on the New York temple, illuminating the city!

Those who profess the Christian religion will occupy the sanctuary, or prayerium, and will be known as the WITNESSES. These will be divided into the SMYRNANS and PHILADELPHIANS, represented by the apocalyptic churches of Smyrna and Philadelphia.

The ECLECTICS are those who occupy the outer courts, and will consist of all those who place themselves under the teachings of Christianity—who enter the Society or CONGREGATION of the TEMPLE, adopt its new style of manners, and who labor to reform business and trade, and carry Christian precepts into practical life,—the object being to concentrate all the GOOD and NOBLE into one grand congregation, and make them useful in improving the surface of the material earth, and in moulding business and the manners of men into harmony with the laws of God!

The greatest education we receive is after going forth into the world of business. The power of *contact with men* and *example* is amazing. Many a man goes home at night with his conscience wounded because he is obliged to do business on worldly principles. The consequence is, his influence on society is lost, while the unscrupulous around him are impressed with the idea that Christianity is a failure. Now we propose separating these from the mass of worldliness by which they are encompassed, and, uniting them, bring their influence to bear directly on society, in diminishing its evils, and increasing its enjoyments, and in improving their own individual characters.

These temples, in the different countries where they are situated, will thus form *nuclei* for these centralizations! Our idea of worship is that it consists of *prayer* and *singing*.

Those who prefer it can therefore worship in their own churches while they join the outer courts, subjecting their business to the jurisdiction of the temple, and enjoying its amusements, and giving their children a temple education—that is, an education with God in it.

There will be two outer courts—an outer and inner or middle,—the first and second courts.

The first court will include those who wish to increase their acquaintance with society, enjoy its amusements, cultivate good manners, and have the advantage of the lectures which they would thus obtain at half the expense that it would otherwise cost them. It is reasonable to suppose that these will be composed, in a large proportion, of young ladies and gentlemen; they will be known as "Palatials," and will wear a hat of a peculiar style, combining taste with comfort.* They can make up, by contributions, a fund for building *a palace* for the grand assemblages.

The second court will include those who subject their business to the jurisdiction and rules of the temple, and thereby put themselves in connection with all the business men of all the temples in different parts of the world.

The object of this is to subject business to such regulations as will protect society against imposition and fraud in its various departments, and give the young man increased advantages in introducing him to the world of business. As this court will necessarily include all those who have great regard for the rights of their fellow-men and the principles of

---

* We call upon the inventive genius of our hatters to furnish such a hat—attractive from its novelty and beauty.

justice, they might be known as JUSTITIANS, or PHILFASIANS, or FASIANS.

The palace should have connected with it all the *amusements* at present known, or new ones, if they can be invented, placed under such restrictions and regulations that young ladies and gentlemen could visit them without those objections which now obtain in connection with the various places of amusements in large cities. This is secured, in the very nature of the institution, in the fact that the palace is placed under the jurisdiction and guidance of the temple, and is frequented only by those who have connected themselves with its outer courts or sanctuary.

The palace will thus become a central rendezvous—place of resort—for men of refinement and cultivation, for literary men (not politicians or demagogues, unless they reform), for the great and good, where the young of both sexes can come in contact with the lights of the age—individuals of moral and intellectual worth—and have their manners formed accordingly, and their moral and intellectual faculties stimulated and strengthened by the intercourse.

An Eclectic, therefore, from Europe, visiting our shores, can, at the palace, come in contact with our best society; and an American Eclectic, visiting Europe, can do the same there; and thus the great minds of the world will be brought into intercourse, and their influence be felt on the rising generation socially, as well as intellectually and morally. A young man from the country, visiting the city, can, at the palace, find plenty of good society and all the amusements he needs, without subjecting himself to the danger of falling into evil company, which now exists in connection with the various places of amusement in our large cities.

The palace should have conversation rooms, assembly rooms, restaurants, and a hotel connected with it, for the accommodation of visitors. A gymnasium, as well as a labyrinth, for am usement and exercise, might also be included.

There might be added a children's court, or a division of the first court, appropriated to juveniles between the ages of four and fourteen years, during which they should be taught the four great scriptural points, and the rudimentary studies necessary to business, and the knowledge of their own language.

EDUCATION.

The highest style of education will be connected with these temples. Considering man as composed of spirit, intellect, imagination, and body, it is necessary that these should be cultivated and improved in harmony with each other.

The spirit is the controlling force. It is depraved, and needs purifying and disciplining.

It can only be purified by the Holy Spirit, sent down from God through the mediation of Jesus Christ.

The spirit, therefore, cannot be educated into *purity*. Depravity is a *quality*, not *ignorance;* it is *filthiness* of nature, and it can only be improved *in quality* by being cleansed with *pure* or *holy spirit* sent down from God. It has a magnetism which is diffused through the blood, and is given off by intercourse with other spirits. Evil is contagious, being a projection of a portion of the evil spirit in a man to other spirits, and so defiling or corrupting it; and goodness is communicated in the same way, and so assists in purifying and cleansing the spirit into which it passes. Hence the value of consociation on the part of good men, that they may mutually and reciprocally contribute to the purification of each other's spiritual natures.

So that a good man who draws down this holy spirit from God imparts it to others without being conscious of it. Every man, therefore, who contends for what is *right—just—*is continually sending off this *pure magnetism*, without being conscious of it, but which has its influence upon others without their having an intelligent understanding of it themselves, but which, if they are evil disposed, they will perceive by the struggle immediately awakened in their own breasts on questions of right and wrong, and which either makes them better or worse.

Connected with the sanctuary will be halls of education. The first the BIBLIUM,* where the scriptures will be taught, particularly with reference to the passions of the human heart, to awakening the conscience through the intellect, teaching the

---

* Some may object to suffixing a Latin termination to an English word. We see no reason why words may not be compounded of different syllables drawn from different languages, as well as sentences be constructed of different words drawn from different languages.

relation man holds to his Maker, and his relations to his fellow. The object will be to popularize and make practical the teachings of scripture on these important points.

The great error of our religious teaching is that the burthen of it is intellectual, and the people are left to grope in the dark as to a thorough knowledge of themselves, or the effect of their own passions on individual happiness and political prosperity.

On the deliverance of the church from the dominion of Pagan Rome, her ministers engaged in the wildest speculations regarding questions of no vital importance to mankind. They tried to inform us, for example, what was the nature of Christ, whether he was compounded or not, or in what manner the union was effected, or whether he was of the same substance with the Father. They undertook to give the world a microscopic view of his body. They tried to settle the subtle question whether his sufferings on the cross were necessary or only occasioned by a submissive act of his will; whether his body was corruptible or incorruptible previous to his resurrection; whether the Deity had three natures or not; whether the world was created by God, or through the instrumentality of angels; and, more difficult still, whether Satan was not the product of chaotic night, and all matter the offspring, as well as the parent, of evil; torturing their brains to find out resemblances between the Platonic and Christian doctrines; how to mystify and discover recondite meanings in scripture, and make the text as unintelligible to others as their discussions were probably unintelligible to themselves; quarreling about the rights of precedence and superiority, and burying the simple worship of the Apostolic Church in magnificence and pomp. These were the great questions about which they bothered themselves during the first few centuries after their deliverance from the power of Pagan Rome; during the feudal ages which succeeded, she was not much better employed; her pretended head was engaged in carrying on struggles with kings and emperors, while the remainder were enlightening the world with the history of saints, and the miracles performed by their relics, and informing us very particularly how many angels could stand on the point of a cambric needle. And, when we consider the change brought about by the Reformation in this particular, what do we find? Why, ourselves involved in learned disquisitions and analyses of *the human un-*

derstanding; the reason, and the origin of IDEAS, whether subjective or objective; whether matter is not a phantasm, and our existence a humbug,—the Aristotelian logic and polemics of the middle ages exploding, as a basis of faith, leaving us surging on the billows of infidelity; settling questions of free will, predestination, and other theological subtleties; analyzing, it is true, with great energy, the chemical ingredients of matter, but, through the whole of these ages, neglecting to analyze and show to the world the passions of the human heart, and the connection between these and the miseries, sufferings, and calamities to which society is subject; on the contrary, glorifying war and the military profession, and thus awakening and stimulating the war spirit in the minds of the young, rather than disgust for it.

It is time the world waked up! The direct tendency of our secular and religious teaching has been to develop principles hostile to Christianity and the good of society. Has man no other mission than that of building himself up? Is not this self-*hood*, of which we have heard so much during the last twenty-five years in our lecture-rooms, in our halls of legislation, and in the discourses of our graduates of colleges on commencement days, a miserable delusion? Does not this isolation of man's sympathies from society disintegrate society? We need a system of teaching which inculcates the thorough dependence of man upon God, and the dependence of each individual of society upon each other. Man's individuality furnishes no element of cohesion to society; such must fall to pieces under pressure, or be held together only by the tremendous machinery of a military force!

The most dangerous passion to society, undoubtedly, is covetousness. We have in preparation an analysis of the passions, which will give some idea of this fearful disease of the soul. Envyings, jealousies, rivalries, ambition and ill-manners spring from it, and it needs being taken in childhood, and a systematic training applied, which will in time weaken and hedge it round by restraining influences, and thus paralyze its action on individuals, communities, and nations.

By making war on this passion, we aim a deadly blow at one evil, which, working quietly, and, more or less, unobserved in its grand effects, is corrupting, disintegrating, and destroying the cohesion of society as much as the lust of gain and lust of power. We mean *marriages* founded *exclusively* upon the union of family inheritances and the desire of riches.

By thus prostituting the sacred passion of love, there is laid a foundation for the prostitution of the body, and the disintegration of the family compact. Light, indeed, has this been esteemed by the Puritan Church, and never been condemned by her; but the hearts that have been desolated by it, the judgment-day only will reveal.

By considering covetousness as a great enemy, to be watched and guarded against, we shall at least diminish the number of such tragedies; and may God help us!

Let it be remembered, that in proportion as man derives enjoyment from the married state, will he defend it; but if he derives no enjoyment from it, he is ready to make war on society generally. Society in England is fast crumbling by a disregard of the marriage relation. By creating a different standard of respectability from that of wealth, we diminish the inducement to its acquisition beyond what is necessary to the comforts of life.

The integral units of society are alienated from each other, and this is the result of covetousness! The absorption of men in business, the expression of their countenances, their acts and manners, all indicate an intense fanaticism, and that of the worst kind—a fanaticism which consumes, as in a burning furnace, the love of letters, the love of good taste, the love of the arts, the love of agreeable manners, dignity, religion, and all the virtues.

It is the source of meanness, ill-breeding, ignorance, want of sociability, cruelty and robbery—whether by pistol or law, makes but little difference.

HISTORICAL EDUCATION.

Next to the BIBLIUM will be the HISTORIUM; one of the most important branches of education connected with the temple will be the study of history. The great object will be to show the sovereignty of God among the nations, and to present the principles and teachings of history. The popular mind should be thoroughly imbued with these teachings, which will be reduced to simple *formulas*, capable of easy acquisition. Mathematics has its formulas. We shall show, in a series of lectures, that history has the same, and that they furnish a beautiful commentary on the truths of revelation. It will be the object of this teaching to show what effect the violation of the *ten commandments* has had upon the destiny of nations by an analysis of all history, and what effect it has upon individuals by biographical statistics collected from men of business.

Adjoining these will be academies of the sciences, in which all the discoveries of science up to the present time will be concentrated. Also, statistics and bureaus of agriculture, fruit raising, manufactures, useful inventions, commerce, trade, and finance, will form a beautiful amphitheatre or court, around the temple which will rise, in the centre, as a glorious symbol of goodness, truth, love and good-will to the nations!

It will be seen that each temple, preserving statistics of the various branches of business in the different countries where they are situated, and having communication with one another, will furnish to the world all the knowledge on these various subjects that can be desired; and the intellect of these countries being directed into useful channels instead of the study of war and the invention of engines of destruction, will benefit the human race.

AGRICULTURE.

The principal business of man should undoubtedly be the cultivation of the soil. There is no nobler pursuit than that of improving and beautifying the earth, to prepare it for its King and Lord. It was intended, on man's expulsion from Eden, that he should cultivate the earth.

Gen. iii. 23: "Therefore the Lord God sent him forth from the garden of Eden, to till the ground from whence he was taken."

The exercise of the physical energy which it necessitates will promote good health and long life. But the department of agricultural industry is only just in its infancy; unimaginable results are yet to be produced by the application of science and from conclusions drawn from statistics on the raising of stock and cultivation of grain and fruits, and it is to be hoped, that by the union and concentration of influence in that direction, to elevate and ennoble that department of industry, and obtain for it precedency over the form of society which gives elevation to the professional classes and the military profession, believing, as we do, that the cultivation of the soil, while it develops the physical energies, is the true source of national wealth and prosperity.

But the witnesses will protest against the corruptions which, in a thousand forms, have penetrated all branches of business. They see nothing but the most detestable criminality in the adulteration of drugs, groceries, dry goods, in false labels, and all "the tricks of trade" that are usually practiced in the various departments of business.

The temples will be a guaranty of the genuineness and value of all those manufactures or articles produced under their jurisdiction and inspection, and according to their rules, and science will consequently be applied to improving fabrics, and not to imposing on the public.

TENTHS.

One-tenth of the income of men of business, where it exceeds their actual wants, should be given to the temple as an annual, voluntary sacrifice to God, which will form a fund, to be appropriated, among other things, to a vast system of charities—to poor and orphans—of which the machinery will be extensive and complete. The idea is to have *a place* for every individual—for the poor boys and girls in the streets of large cities*—for wealthy young men, who are not under the necessity of doing business—and for octogenarians who wish to retire from business and devote the remainder of their days to something useful. It will be shown that the following law or principle controls the history of nations and the business of individuals, viz.: that "God requires a sacrifice; if made, the individual or nation gets credit for it; if not, He takes it, and the individual gets no credit for it."

It will be shown, by statistics gathered from men of business, that every man between the years of twenty and sixty loses more than one-tenth of his property by casualties and

---

* It ought to be recollected that it is from this class that our burglars, pick-pockets, thieves, garroters, and bullies proceed, and then the wisdom of having the temple extend its influence to them will be seen.

mishaps; in other words, God takes it from him, and in ninety-five cases out of a hundred strips him entirely! In other words, business done on the *selfish* principle has *a law* working against success, which, in ninety-five cases out of a hundred, brings ruin.

At the age of sixty the Eclectic will retire from business. Those who attain this period without the requisite means of subsistence will be sustained from the funds of the temple. If they die before that time, without property, the widow and children, if any, will be provided for from the same source. It will thus be seen that the fear and dread of future poverty will thus be removed from the mind, and a compromise be effected between the spirit of covetousness and the spirit of benevolence, much to the advantage of society and the individual himself.

The concentration of vast capital in the hands of a few, to be wielded against smaller capitalists, will thus be remedied in a great measure; and, although some opposition for this reason may be anticipated from this source, it must be endured.

MANNERS.

The style of American manners is exceedingly objectionable. It has nothing in it of the spirit of Christianity. Christianity commands us to be gentle, and a man that is gentle is a *gentleman*. To love our neighbor as ourselves requires that our regards should be extended to our fellow-man with reference to this world, as well as the next; and this should be expressed in social life, and in our intercourse with each other.

Why should French politeness be superior to that of the Christian?

Why should West Point turn out more agreeable manners than our theological seminaries? Because the military man is more Christian in his deportment than the professor of religion; because the atheistic Frank illustrates the Christian precept, "Do unto others as you would be done by," more than the believer in Christianity, whose author made that command one of the cardinal virtues of his religion!

Where else can be found that anomalous compound of egoism and smooth or brusk assumption of authority that ever seems to dwell about the persons of some of our Protestant clergymen? We do not say all—there are exceptions; but then there should be no exceptions in cases of this kind.

Those who are not so, are entitled to more honor.

Pride of intellect, jealousy, and envy of one another's superiority or success, are among the monstrous sins of which some of them are guilty!*

The scriptures require the crucifixion of our evil desires, not the love of the beautiful and the artistic; and why should not this be expressed through the dress and manners, as well as on the face of nature?

Surely, Puritans had not the management of the material creation; if they had, it would not have been made so beautiful and attractive; and God has nowhere forbidden us to look upon and enjoy it. The development of our love of the beautiful and art, employs the faculties, and prevents the strengthening of the more sordid passions of our nature, and, therefore, it should be encouraged and indulged in.

Mercantile manners, formed behind the counter, are not much better—rudeness and audacity combined, that seems to regard men as bales of goods to be fumbled over—if profitable, laid hold of; if not, thrown aside as worthy of no further notice.

What is it that makes the manners of children so attractive? All love them. All are charmed by them. And yet no one seems to imagine there is any thing here that can be imitated! And yet Christ tells us that unless we become as little children we cannot see the kingdom of God!

Our national manners are unchristian in the extreme, and should be reformed! The people want urbanity, frankness, and confidence in one another.

AMUSEMENTS.

Amusements, as well as music, are medicinal. New and attractive ones will be invented for all classes—for the young

---

* Some professors of religion, particularly if they have wealth, think themselves justified in putting all sorts of impertinent questions to those who happen to be introduced to them by letter—a breach of good manners not allowable among gentlemen; and we are not aware that the Bible authorizes any such conduct; on the contrary, rebukes it, for this is not courtesy, but the assumption of authority over another.

and for the old. The nervous systems of men of business are being crushed for the want of them.

The roofs of buildings in our large cities might be used for pedestrians to pass to and fro about the city, away from the dust and jostling of the crowd and rattle of vehicles in the streets below! Wire bridges might be used for crossing from one roof to another. Our railroads might be constructed—and they will be sometime—on a larger and more commodious principle! The cars will be broad and spacious, with splendid apartments elegantly furnished, with culinary arrangements and sleeping-rooms as convenient and comfortable as those of a fine hotel, and their motion so easy and pleasant as to be scarcely perceptible!

A large portion of the diseases and ailings of society are the result of the want of proper *exhilaration* of the brain and the nerves, the cherishing of morbid passions, and the want of physical exercise in the open air! It will be found that the mind craves those amusements which have a certain amount of strife or rivalry in them, which, in this case, there can be no objection to; the amusements of children run into this. This kind seems most to electrify and excite the brain and the nervous system, and, consequently, are the more healthful and invigorating to body and mind!

A class of amusements will be invented, founded on this principle, and we call upon the genius of our countrymen to help along in this matter.

A series of annual festivals will be instituted after the ripening of fruits, in which there will be a grand assemblage of all American Eclectics at the principal temple. Of course, there must necessarily be a large multitude, male and female, varying from four years old and upward, and they will form magnificent processions, with beautiful dresses and fine music. A feast of fruits in the palace will be held at the same time. This will be national. But the grandest and most beautiful festival of all will be the one every five years, if that period should be deemed desirable, in which the nationalities of all the world will be assembled, each nation represented by its peculiar garb and insignia—the Irish, Scotch, English, French, German, Italian, Turkish, Russian, all with their magnificent choirs of music, shaking the very heavens with their hosannas!

THE HEBREW RACE.

It is believed that the Jewish race will yet prove the conservators of society, and that the Gentile race will be compelled to give up its dominion, and that it will go down with a crash of nations that will make the universe shudder at the noise of it!

Jerusalem will be rebuilt and repossessed by the Jews, and will become the metropolis of the earth and the center of civilization and commerce; and the great wave of civilization which is now passing across this continent is only part of the process designed to bring about that event, and when this wave shall have circumscribed the globe, and shall approach Jerusalem from the west, and from the east, then that city will begin to be possessed by the Jews. Every railroad built, every steamer constructed on the Pacific, every blow struck on our immense prairies, will only hasten that event! This is the reason of the frenzy of men in building railroads and steamers, and clearing away forests and occupying land; they know not whence it proceeds, but it proceeds from God, who is making use of their enthusiasm to accomplish His purposes—to make rough places smooth and to prepare a *highway* for our God!

GOVERNMENT AND LAW.

At the age of sixty, the Eclectic having retired from business, now, having the advantage of age and experience, becomes a prince or judge of the temple, and wears a badge, and dresses accordingly.

A class will thus be formed, who, having ample leisure and experience, and having passed the period when ambition is the most powerful in the human breast, will have liberty to give their attention to works of usefulness. To them all difficult questions arising in the temple will be submitted for adjudication.

These adjudications will be based on two principles—one on that of right and justice, and the other on that of protecting the weak and ignorant against the strong—superior intelligence and sharpness.

The monstrous absurdity of supposing a thing is right because it *is legal*, will be repudiated!

Robbery by law, therefore, will not be sanctioned.

The principle that no individual will *willingly* or *knowingly* deprive himself of his rights, will be adopted, and no signed or sealed instrument, therefore, which does this, ought to be recognized!

The legal maxim, "caveat emptor," will not obtain in the temple.

No man desires to cheat himself and no law will be so administered as to make him do so!

The law of "adverse possession" and all "statutes of limitation" will, consequently, be ignored.

A man can never lose his rights except by crime. No valuable consideration will do; there must be an *equivalent* consideration either in *property* or *friendship*.

The Palatial never having advanced further than the first court, will not be entitled to become a prince or judge, as none but those who have made some sacrifice for the public good will be so honored.

MUSIC.

Talent for music will be cultivated. Musicians from all parts of the world should be sought after and made serviceable for worship, amusements, and medicine.

The effect of music upon the nervous system is not sufficiently considered by our modern philanthropists. Its influence over diseases is quite overlooked, though the ancients knew something of it; the infidel will not be moved by the story of David curing Saul with his harp, but he will be by the account of Homer representing the Grecian army as employing music to stay the raging of the plague, and Pindar's statement that Æsculapius healed acute diseases with soothing songs. Pliny does not credit the recommendation of Theophrastus, who suggests a tune for the cure of the hip gout, and laughs at the idea (as well he might) entertained by Cato that music would set a limb that was out of joint, and which, Varro declares, was good for the gout. But shall the statement of Aulus Gellius, who cites a work of Theophrastus, be accepted, which recommends music as a specific for the bite of a viper?

Boyle and Shakspeare did not disbelieve in the effect of

music *supervesicam;* and Kircher's Musurgia and Swinburn's Travels relate its effects on those who were bitten by the tarantula!

Even the imperturbable Sir William Temple seems to give credit to the stories of the power of music over diseases; but it is refreshing to hear the lively Vigneul de Marville confidently affirm that music and the sounds of musical instruments contribute to the health of body and mind, assist the circulation of the blood, and increase the action of the excretory organs; and no modern physician will deny the effect of music upon the nervous system when his reputation for capacity might be questioned by every mother while she sings her child to sleep.

Music awakens courage and enthusiasm on the field of battle; it gave the soldiers of Napoleon increased energy to surmount the Alps; it will charm animals, and soothe into repose the lunatic!

Let us have more of it and of a better sort,—none of your operatic kind, which has appeared to distort all that is refined and elevated in harmony, and which requires a cultivated taste to appreciate—no doubt; all violations of good taste do, for it has to displace that before it can be substituted in its stead,—like tobacco and ardent spirits, unnatural at first, and sickening, but gradually creating for itself an artificial and depraved appetite. This barbarous style of music, the greatest evidence we have in modern times of the want of soul in man, which takes the judgment by storm, and produces astonishment which some mistake for admiration, is founded on a great law of depravity, and that is, that it loves noise. The exaggerated chant of the Roman church, rendered more horrible by intensification, was originally forced into popularity by being associated with the royal marriage of Henry IV., of France, and subsequently by the patronage of Louis XIV.; thus commanding the patronage of courtiers and aristocracy, who probably thought more of viewing the beauties of the court and high dames through their opera glasses than they did of listening to the performers on the stage, who were screaming to get up a sensation. This depraved style of music is insinuating itself into our churches, perverting all that is venerable! Let those who admire it enjoy it; for ourselves, we make no pretensions that way!

TEACHERS.

La Monnoye has a note as follows: "The hall of the school of equity, at Poitiers, where the Institutes were read, was called La Ministerie, on which head Florimond de Remond—book 7, c. 11—speaking of Albert Babinot, one of the first disciples of Calvin, after having said he was called 'the good man,' adds, that because he had been a student of the Institutes at this Ministerie of Poitiers, Calvin and others styled him Mr. Minister, from whence, afterwards, Calvin took occasion to give the name of ministers to the pastors of his churches."

Florimond de Remond overlooked the fact, that the word is employed by the apostle on several occasions: 2 Cor. iii., 6, 7, where he speaks of the "able ministers of the New Testament;" and it would appear, from 2 Cor. vi., that all believers are considered as the "ministers of God;" and in Romans xiii. rulers are termed "God's ministers."

1 Cor. xii., 28: "And God hath set some in the church. First, apostles; second, prophets; third, teachers; after that, miracles; then gifts of healing, helps, governments, diversities of tongues."

Eph. iv., 11: "And he gave some apostles, and some prophets, and some evangelists, and some pastors and teachers."

In the Church of Antioch there were "prophets and teachers."

There will be connected with each sanctuary TEACHERS, whose duty it shall be to teach the scriptures. These teachers will be selected from those who have been educated at the Temple, and on account of their peculiar qualifications and fitness for the business, and not from favoritism or influence beyond that.

In secular education, books should be rather for the teachers than the scholars, and education should be orally conducted. The custom of giving children tasks to perform, with the command, "study it out," we consider pernicious, besides a great waste of energy and time. The ambitious overwork their youthful brains and bring on nervous diseases which last during the rest of their lives, while the dull ones become discouraged by their inability to accomplish their task, and either shirk it, or call upon their classmates to furnish that explanation which should have been furnished by their teachers. All subjects have to be presented differently to different minds, and this can only be done by the teacher studying the nature of the mind he has to deal with, addressing himself accordingly. Dreary and unlovely are the visions which crowd upon our minds as we dwell upon the early years of our educational life; cold stone walls, dusty, dirty, chilling, with indented, battered oak stairs, leading to rooms reminding one of garrets in some old store-house, or the dungeons of a prison, rather than halls of science, so that it is difficult to allude to it without a feeling of humiliation. No wonder the great mass of those who were thus treated like animals have become worse, and inflicted on society corresponding disrespect.

By having banks connected with the temples, may they not be made to furnish a balance or center of gravity to the world's financial machinery—a thing absolutely necessary to the commerce of nations, and one of the yet unsolved problems of finance?

We call upon the young and beautiful minds of America, and of other nations, to come forth and unite themselves. Never was there a higher and more glorious mission than that which now offers itself to them,—that of saving society from the demon of evil, and themselves from the corruptions and delusions which are pressing upon them on all sides!

Communi
addressed to the Latarg

A Register will be opened, for the names of Palatials and others, at the Fifth Avenue Hotel, or some other prominent place, of which due notice will be given.

PROGRAMME OF LECTURES.

J. B. HOLGATE,—

Dear Sir : The undersigned having examined your analysis of history, and convinced of its importance to the public, would respectfully suggest to you its application to popular lectures. The simplicity and comprehensiveness of the system renders the entire field of history accessible to the public—a desideratum long felt by European scholars. America should feel proud of this achievement.

It is not a distaste for history, but the want of suitable aids for its acquisition, that renders Americans generally so neglectful of this branch of knowledge. With the facilities furnished by your labors, however, we have no doubt a more general interest will be manifested in the subject. In furtherance of this object we would recommend to you the delivery of public lectures in the various cities of the Union.

Signed,
GEORGE ALLEN, Prof. of Ancient Languages in the University of Pennsylvania.
ALONZO POTTER, Bishop of the Prot. Epis. Church, Pa.
CHAS. HENRY, Late Prof. of Philosophy and History in the University of the City of New York.
JARED SPARKS, Late President of Harvard University.
CHAS. KING, President of Columbia College.
SAM'L. R. JOHNSON, Prof. of Syst. Div. Gen'l Theological Seminary.
THOMAS HOUSE TAYLOR, Rector Grace Church, N. Y.
MILLARD FILLMORE, Ex-President U. S. A.
HORACE WEBSTER, New York Free Academy.

It was in consequence of the foregoing letter, which was initiated by the late Prof. Hackley, of Columbia College, that we were induced to go on and finish our system, and we have not till the present moment been prepared to bring it before the public. It has taken more time than we anticipated to complete it.

We shall present the old Assyrian Empire, Hebrew, Medo-Persian, Greek and Roman histories, with that dark epoch in European history, the breaking up of the Roman Empire by the barbarians. Also, subsequent European events with the Arabians and Turks, and the overthrow of the Eastern Empire. The Royal families of Europe—the Merovingians, Carlovingians, Capetians, Bourbons, Hapsburghs, Hohenzollerns, Plantaganets, Stuarts, and Napoleons—with the great European wars and development of States, will be considered. The main object will be to show the connection of events and *epochs* with, and their dependence upon, each other; furnishing a key to the *elements*, *forces*, and *laws* of history; developing *principles* which will be profitable to society and individuals.

We believe we have discovered the great law—that law which is the same to history that gravitation is to matter, and which the world has long been seeking for—and shall at a proper time announce it. These lectures, therefore, will present a system of history entirely novel and original, of which the world has not hitherto had any knowledge, founded on a philosophical analysis which the judgment will recognize as simple and appropriate.

It will be found that society is struggling in the face of some fundamental laws which, rather than yield to it, will crush it first.

It will be found that history is not a medley of accidents, as is imagined by some, but is connected by principles from the remotest periods of time, all chained together by *cause* and *effect*, and directed towards a given result, which is the great problem of history.

POPULAR COURSE—ASSYRIAN AND BABYLONIAN.

FIVE LECTURES—$2.00.

1. ORIGIN OF RACES.
2. THE FOUR GREAT CULMINATIONS.—THE HEBREWS.
3. THE MONARCHY AND DIVISION.
4. THE ASSYRIAN EMPIRE.
5. THE BABYLONIAN EMPIRE.

Only enough of this history will be given to present the great epochs in their connexion with subsequent history—a more full and minute detail being furnished in the biblical course.

GRECIAN HISTORY.

TICKETS—$2.50.

1. FIRST COLONIZATION OF GREECE.—THE JAVANICS, PELASGI AND HELLENES.
2. ATHENS.—ITS CONNEXION WITH XERXES' INVASION OF GREECE.
3. THE PELOPONNESIAN WAR.—CONNEXION WITH THE PRECEDING SHOWN.
4. MACEDON.—PHILIP.—THE CONNEXION BETWEEN THE FOREGOING EPOCHS SHOWN.
5. ALEXANDER THE GREAT.—OVERTHROW OF THE PERSIAN EMPIRE.
6. DIVISION OF ALEXANDER'S EMPIRE.—THE PTOLEMICS AND SELEUCIDAE.

ROMAN HISTORY.

TICKETS—$2.50.

1. ROMAN HISTORY.—FIRST COLONIZATION OF ITALY.—THE MONARCHY.
2. THE REPUBLIC.
3. THE PUNIC WARS.
4. CIVIL WARS OF THE REPUBLIC.
5. EMPIRE.—(The principles developed in the last two lectures important.)
6. DIOCLESIAN AND CONSTANTINE.—(Change of the Roman Constitution.)

TWENTY-FIVE LECTURES ON EUROPEAN HISTORY.

(Forming part of the Metropolitan Course.)

TICKETS TO THE COURSE—$10.00.

Lecture 1. INROADS OF THE BARBARIANS.
" 2. CLOVIS.—FOUNDING OF THE FRENCH MONARCHY.—ITS CONNEXION WITH THE PRESENT TIME SHOWN.
" 3. CHARLEMAGNE LAYS THE FOUNDATION OF MODERN EUROPEAN TROUBLES.
" 4. CAPETS.—FEUDAL SYSTEM.
" 5. BOURBONS.
" 6. THE CARLOVINGIANS IN GERMANY.—OTHO I.—THE SAXON EMPERORS.
" 7. THE SALIC EMPERORS.—HILDEBRAND.—THE GREAT STRUGGLE.
" 8. THE HAPSBURGHS.
" 9. THE REFORMATION.
" 10. THE THIRTY YEARS' WAR.
" 11. SPAIN.—THE VISIGOTHS AND SARACENS.
" 12. NAPLES.—THE NORMANS.
" 13. THE BOURBONS IN SPAIN AND NAPLES.
" 14. THE SARACENS.
" 15. THE TURKS.
" 16. THE HOHENZOLLERNS.
" 17. FREDERICK THE GREAT.—PRUSSIA.

Lecture 18. RUSSIA.—TERRITORIAL EXPANSION.
" 19. BRITAIN.—CELTS.
" 20. THE NORMANS.
" 21. ENGLAND.—THE SECULAR CIVIL WARS AND WARS WITH FRANCE.
" 22. THE RELIGIOUS CIVIL WARS.
" 23. ENGLAND.—1688.—CURIOUS PROCESS GOING ON IN ENGLISH TERRITORIAL POSSESSIONS
" 24. ENGLAND.—MARATIME WARS.
" 25. NAPOLEONS.—BOURBONS AND HAPSBURGHS. — Important as showing what is now developing in Europe.

These lectures, with the exception of the minor European course, including some supplementary lectures, will form the METROPOLITAN or full popular course. It will consist of from 55 to 60 lectures, and will be delivered one or two each week, as may be desired. There will be an afternoon course also to accommodate those who cannot attend evenings.

Included among the Supplementary Lectures will be several entitled "CHAINS," viz. :

THE MEDIAN CHAIN.
THE NORMAN.
THE HOHENZOLLERN.
THE TEUTONIC KNIGHT'S CHAIN, ILLUSTRATIVE OF THE SUPERMENTAL FORCE.

A SUPPLEMENTARY LECTURE, SHOWING A PROVIDENCE IN THE BOURBON DYNASTY, THE RESULT OF A SINGULAR ANALYSIS.

Tickets to the course—$25.00. Single Tickets—50 cents.

MINOR POPULAR COURSE OF TWELVE LECTURES ON EUROPEAN HISTORY.

Tickets to this Course—$5.00.

Lecture 1. BARBARIANS.
" 2. CLOVIS.
" 3. CHARLEMAGNE.
" 4. CAPETS.—FEUDAL SYSTEM.—CRUSADES.—BOURBONS.
" 5. GERMANY.
" 6. NAPLES.
" 7. HAPSBURGHS.
" 8. PRUSSIA.
" 9. RUSSIA.
" 10. ARABIANS.—TURKS.
" 11. SPAIN.
" 12. EUROPE SINCE 1815 (important as showing what is developing on the Continent at the present time).

A PRIVATE FULL COURSE.

We have also concluded to give to a few, who may desire it, a full course of the WORLD'S HISTORY, taking up the details, presenting a view of battles, characters of great men, the policies of cabinets, forms of governments, civil and religious institutions, inventions and their effect on society, commerce and literature in all their varied relations, connections, and bearings upon each other, accompanied with drawings representing royal families, intermarriages, and consequently the clues to many of the great wars, epochs, phases, chains, synchronological relations, &c., &c. This will occupy one year, five lessons a week, and will be $500.

A PRIVATE COURSE.

A private course will also be delivered, giving a view of the great phases, pivots, and principles, designed to be more condensed and full than the popular course. $1.00 a Lecture.

This is the course alluded to in the letter of our Consul to Hamburg.

A biblical course, didactical, historical, and prophetical, on the Sabbath. Annual subscription—$10.00.

Also, a course of six lectures, giving the four scriptural points or pivots which should be universally understood. Tickets to the course—$1.00; single, 25 cents.

From John B. Miller, the United States Consul at Hamburg.

"Having enjoyed the pleasure and benefit of listening to part of your lectures, I desire to express to you the satisfaction they have afforded me.

"The result of my previous reading on European history had left but confused and vague impressions upon this complicated portion of the world's history. I attended thirty-two of your lectures, and they have reduced this chaos to lucid order, and I now feel that the relief afforded to my mind upon subjects which would otherwise have ever remained in a state of confusion and obscurity is of the very highest utility and value to me. I consider myself very fortunate in having had the opportunity of hearing them.

"N. B.—Should you visit Germany in your European travels I hope you will make it a point to come to Hamburg and deliver a course of your lectures there. I should like to attend a complete course myself, and will do what I can to aid in so useful a work."

From the Albany Argus.

"Mr. Holgate is a gentleman who has traveled and seen mankind extensively in his own and in foreign countries. He studies languages as a philosophical etymologist rather than a parsing grammarian, not negligent of grammatical proprieties and accuracy, but searching into the radical elements of words, and tracing their variations of present meaning in their multiform uses. He has studied hard and perseveringly and deserves the merit of a sound and ripe scholar, though his modest and unobtrusive nature holds him back from all ostentation of learning. He should have placed in his hands the amplest means of prosecuting his elevated plans for the enlightenment of his country, for which he possesses qualifications of a high order."

From JARED SPARKS, *to* HENRY STEVENS, ESQ., *London.*

"He has devoted several years to the construction of a series of historical Charts, which are executed not only with great labor of research, but with remarkable skill, accuracy, and completeness, and are equally well adapted to the English and American market."

From REV. G. W. HOSMER, *July* 2, 1860.

"It gives me great pleasure to introduce to you my old friend, J. B. Holgate, Esq., recently returned from Europe, and for more than twenty years an investigator of history. He has important works ready to come before the public—one of great magnitude on the World's History, and at this time is publishing the first volume of a series which I know will interest you.* The world will be benefited by his indefatigable industry and world-wide investigations."

The same writer, at a much earlier date, speaking of Mr. Holgate's scheme of history, says: "He has done a good work for the *Church* and the *World.*" This gentleman is still living, and we have no doubt will be pleased to learn the splendid results which have flown from Mr. Holgate's labors and which he seems to have foreseen.

Over twenty years ago Mr. Holgate brought to New York City the specimen drawing of his scheme of history, and the following testimonials will show those who have not been acquainted with his labors the opinion entertained of them by the learned:

From COUNT CASTELNAU, *Member of the Royal Geog. Soc. of France.*

"*Mon Cher Monsieur,*—D'apres votre désir j'ai examiné avec soin votre

* Noachidae.

Belle Carte et je crois seulement lui rendre justice en disant que par le nombre de faits quelle contient et l'ordre systematique dans lequel ils sont rangé elle est infiniment superieure a tous les ouvrages de meme nature que j'ai vus soit en France soit en Angleterre."

[*Translation of the above.*]

"In accordance with your wish, I have carefully examined your admirable Chart, and think it but justice to say that, considering the amount of material it contains and the lucid method in which it is arranged, I have seen no work, either in France or in England, that can compare with it in these respects."

The Rev. Hanson Cox thus expresses himself:—"It is a learned, ingenious, and valuable invention, to which the author has devoted much assiduity, and is in a high degree an original performance. It is a native production from a mind young though rich and comparatively mature, and seems to claim with energy, as well as modesty, the appreciation and patronage of his countrymen."

From Lt.-Gov. Bradish, *to* Gov. Everett, *of Massachusetts:*

"I cannot but regard this work as a new and valuable addition to the means of general knowledge. As such, I feel confident that the deep interest you have ever evinced in the great cause of civilization, as well as the effective efforts you have contributed towards its promotion, will lead you to hail with pleasure, and to regard with favor, the labors of Mr. Holgate."

Mr. Bradish lived just long enough to see Mr. Holgate's labors culminate, but not to witness their full fruit.

From the late Rev. Dr. Brownlee *to the* Rev. Dr. Breckenridge:

"I introduce to you the bearer, Mr. Holgate, the author of a most interesting historical and chronological chart on a new model.

"Be pleased to say a good word for an ingenious scholar, who deserves well of his country and the church by his most useful labors in those fields."

The *North American Review*, speaking of the same drawings, says: "They will probably come into extensive use."

A gentleman, writing to Senator Sumner, 1863, speaking of the completed drawings, says: "It seems to me to be a work beneficial to mankind."

From the Rev. W. R. Whittingham, D. D., *Professor of Church History in the Genl. Theol. Sem. of the Prot. Epis. Ch., N. Y.*

"I have much pleasure in expressing my sense of the neatness, simplicity, and uncommon combination of these characteristics, with the copiousness and minuteness of Mr. Holgate's chart of history. I do not remember any similar chart that can be compared with it in these respects. A child may be taught to use it, while the finished scholar may consult it with satisfaction. The combination of geography, ethnography, chronology, with biography, literary history, and a judicious selection of facts of general history, sacred and profane, is so complete and yet so simple as to be very remarkable."

Booksellers and publishers are interested in the success of these lectures, for by creating a taste for history we produce a demand for books.

Newspapers, Journals, and Reviews are interested in the success of these lectures, for they are our only sources of current history, and they will be demanded for a similar reason.

But the property men of the country are interested in their success as aiming to develop the intellect, and connecting our internal emotions with political and practical life, and exhibiting the connexion between our passions and the prosperity and downfall of governments, and consequently the stability of society, and on the principle that an intelligent man contributes more to the value of property than an ignorant one.

The pulpit is interested in their success as showing a God in history.

These lectures will be commenced at Room No. 24, Cooper Institute.

www.ingramcontent.com/pod-product-compliance
Lightning Source LLC
LaVergne TN
LVHW011136110826
845150LV00008B/2372

* 9 7 8 1 4 1 8 1 9 4 5 4 3 *